DYNAMIC TRANSITIONS

How To Move Boldly And Gracefully
Into The Next Great Phase Of Your Life

By

Dr Wayne D Pernell

Be sure to get your Bonus Material here:
www.DynamicTransitions.com/bonus

ISBN-13: 978-0998146126
ISBN-10: 0998146129

To reach out to Dr Wayne Pernell for speaking or world-class coach-ing and advising for your organization, executive team, division, work team, or yourself as an individual leader looking to invest in a commitment to your personal and professional growth, please write to Wayne@DynamicLeader.com. You may use the same address for ordering bulk copies of Dynamic Transitions (or any of Dr Pernell's other books).

Because of the dynamic nature of the Internet, web addresses or links contained in this book may have changed since publication and may no longer be valid. The author of this book does not dispense medical, legal, or psychological advice, nor does he suggest any technique as a form of treatment for medical, physical, or emotional problems. Always consult the appropriate professional. The intent of the author is solely to provide information of a general nature to aid the reader in attaining a greater perspective for personal and professional growth. No guarantees of growth are implied or promised. Your use of the information in this book for yourself is your responsibility and your actions and the author assumes no responsibility or liability for the outcome of those actions.

WHY THIS BOOK?

Dr Wayne Pernell, known for his expertise in the areas of relationships and leadership development and given the moniker of "The Leaders' Leader," has done it again. Who isn't in a transition of some sort. In this International Best-Selling work, Dynamic Transitions walks the reader through the process of identifying values, letting go of the past, and stepping into a bright, glorious future.

Think about where you were last year or even last week. You are in transition in at least a couple areas of your life. If you are honest, you know you need this book.

As a serial entrepreneur and cancer survivor, I have had plenty of my own transitions. My identity has been challenged many times along the way as a business owner, father, and human.

What about you?

Dynamic Transitions is for you. And, by the way, Dr Wayne Pernell is a great guy, too.

Mike Koenigs
Serial Entrepreneur, TV Show Host,
Author, Speaker, and Disruptasaurus

DEDICATION

For Shannon who, as my loving partner, shows up as my muse with both support and inspiration for me on our delightfully wacky journey together.

This is quite a ride! It's all love and monkeys and we're just getting started!

Jacob, Lucas, Daniella, Sarina, and Trinity each serve to inspire and support me and my work, as well. The funny thing is that they may not even know the tremendous role they each play in my life and therefore in my work.

We're there for each other and you have my love and gratitude.

ACKNOWLEDGMENTS

Beyond the dedication, this work could not come about without the support and love of my wife, Shannon. My exclamations of, "Hey, I have an idea!" are always met with inquiries about what the ideas are and, without judgment or hesitation, the reasons that I *have to* pursue them. Who else is blessed with *that* kind of support?

My gratitude goes to Ms. Tami Mize, my editor. She is able to juggle multiple projects and deadlines and with grace, take on one more.

So much appreciation continues to go to Everett O'Keefe who guided my progress and gently kept me on track.

Dynamic Transitions became an *International #1 Best-Seller* the day of its pre-launch. Only through the support and teachings about framework and business from such great mentors as Brendon Burchard, Mike Koenigs, Ed Rush, and their teams could I dream of (and be pushed to) producing more and serving more greatly. (Mike Koenigs gets an extra hug – verbally and virtually here – for being the gentle-yet-direct beautiful soul that he is.)

I have so much gratitude for the VIP-members of the mastermind groups to which I belong who continue to reach out in support, creating a net across the globe.

My dad's message of "Do Good Stuff" continues to propel me forward, as well. My mom's belief in me continues to surround me like a warm hug.

For all of these, and so much more, I am grateful.

FOREWORD

When a room of 100 people had a question posed, all but two or three of them raised their hands and that was because they were distracted by something else (computer, phone, etc.).

The question: *Who here is in some form of transition right now? Whether it's in your personal life, your relationship, your career, your financial status, your living situation, or your spiritual connection, who here is in some form of transition?*

That is 100% of us. One... hundred... percent of us are in some form of transition right now. And, we always will be. A transition isn't an event. A transition is a process.

And that process is life. We're continually in transition. That doesn't end. We just move from transition to transition and from phase to phase of life. The trick is to do so gracefully. The joy is in doing so boldly and truly owning your life as you do.

So c'mon! Step into your Dynamic Transition and enjoy moving boldly and gracefully into the next great phase of your life!

AUTHOR'S NOTE TO READERS

We all move through time, or perhaps it moves through us. And, things change. The things around us change. Our circumstances change. And we change.

Knowing how that happens will make a big difference in your life.

As with my other books, I have written this in a conversational style. While this page is the only one in which you'll find a first-person reference, I think you'll appreciate that we're just talking.

I'm your coach and advisor. I'm your trainer, too. I'll walk you through what's necessary to get you from an idea, through turmoil, and out the other side.

You're already in transition. Are you ready to take it on and come through it with boldness and grace? Let's do this! Read on and we'll talk!

~ Dr P ~

CONTENTS

1

THE NATURE OF TRANSITIONS

We inhale. We exhale. And the last breath is gone... until we take another. And we DO take another, and another, until we don't.

So often, people think of transitions as simply related to retirement. But the nature of transitions is so much more than that. Transitions is about moving across any major stage of our lives. We move from childhood to adulthood. We cross over from being single to being in a couple or family. And we change course in our lives from working to doing something different. We let go of the role we had in a job to become someone new. We let go of a relationship in one form to have it take on a new form. We watch our bank accounts and our waistlines grow and shrink, each day knowing they too are in transition. And we take steps to manage them as they reflect a piece of our lives, an outer reference to our personal identities.

Transitions are about your personal identity.

The book you are now holding, Dynamic Transitions, is about you taking charge of who you are becoming in the world. This is YOUR world. How do you want to show up in it? Wouldn't you love to feel like you own it again? Yes, it's time to move gracefully, yet boldly, into the next great phase of your life.

From a cellular level to an emotional and existentially philosophical level, we face transitions every moment of every day. In the blink of an eye, quite literally, we are no longer who we were. Who we have been got us to who we are now. And who we have been can be only a memory at this point.

From the Latin, "trans" means across or to cross. The nature of transitions, then, is that we are moving from one place to another. We move across or cross over from where we have been to where we are going and end up NOW. There is irony here because transitions are active. We are in the process of moving. The odd thing is, we measure our feelings based on the experience of the moment.

It is precisely that which makes transitions so difficult and why we end up fearing change so greatly. *We can only experience the now.* We project forward into the unknown and, without definitive outcomes, we imagine what might be. We worry about what is to come. In the absence of information, we make things up. Therefore, when we think about our future, especially when it's based on letting go of what we know, we tend to catastrophize. We believe that nothing could be as good as what we had.

Oh sure, we hope it *will* be. But we fret over what *might* be.

And truly, transitions are about letting go of the past and creating something new for the future. Transitions are about building bridges in time. That means that you are in transitions every moment of every day.

Now your task is to be in that bridging place, that place of NOW, very deliberately and intentionally. Deliberately means that you are choosing to put yourself into the space of bridge-building from the past to the future. Intentionally means that you have a focus and clarity about who you are and where you are going.

Just as when remodeling a house, there are some features that you will want to keep. There are some that you will want to enhance. There are some features that will need to go. Throughout it all, there will be dust. There may be tears. But there is a positive outcome based on a plan. Get it? You will be letting go of some things, building on others, and working toward something specific. No one does a remodel without a plan.

How will you move gracefully and boldly into your future? You do this by reflecting on what is working for you, what you want to take with you, what you want to (or need to) leave behind, and continuing to focus on where you are headed. Through it all, there will be noise (a lot of people will tell you what you "should" be doing). There will be dust (as old pieces of your history come to light, you will shake them off to view them anew). And there may be tears. Again, as you review the history of who you have been, you may engage in mourning what was.

The tears may come from overwhelm, as well. When faced with a transition, even when it is planned, such a shift may seem to come in a rush. When embracing (or confronting) a transition, the details of the next action steps can feel over-whelming. There are too many things to track as "to-be-done." These serve to distract, however, since the true work of transitions is very personal and somewhat emotional.

Chaos is common. Expect to feel it. And, when you can welcome it, knowing that the remodel of this phase of your life has a plan and a desired outcome state, you can gently – and perhaps eagerly – work toward that.

It is with one foot in each world of both the past and the future, that you boldly venture forth. It is as the dust settles that you tidy up. You heal, seal, and install anew. And then you employ your skills and new tools to pursue your new path.

Dynamic Transitions is about building your skills. From time to time you will need to reflect on your current competencies. In so doing you can then step into your broader capacity. Here, you will begin to get a little clearer about where you're headed. To do so, you need to become a lot clearer about your own style of how you brace against or embrace the world currently. There is really no judgment here. At times, both styles are essential. Seldom is a person all one or the other style in all circumstances.

So be you. Take a look at the questions that follow. As you do, and to get the most out of this book, take some time to reflect on how each of the topics actually, truly, really does show up in your life.

As a bonus to having gotten this far, you may choose to visit www.DynamicTransitions.com/bonus to download a somewhat expanded version of the following assessment and guide. Provided here for you to give it some thought, you will find it valuable to go through this exercise and actually put pen to paper. Where there are blanks, fill them in. Where there is a Y/N, answer honestly. It's not an extreme polar measure of all or nothing. Think of it like a scale; if you're even slightly leaning one way or the other, then you just call it what it is. This is simply a different way of doing a 1-5 scale. This is for you. If you're leaning lower, it's a No. If you're leaning higher, it's a Yes. Both are okay. Again, this is to get you thinking about your life right now. You are, with full intention, going to step into it, recapture it, and create the future you desire. So, where are you now?

- When I awaken every day, I set the intention of being (how) _____.

- I am clear about my intentions in my interactions with other people: Y/N

- My outcomes seldom match my initial intentions in my interactions with others: Y/N

- I am absolutely certain that I can create the situations I need to be successful: Y/N

- I set the standards for success in my life: Y/N

- I actually feel pretty comfortable with where I'm heading: Y/N

- To tell the truth, I'm pretty anxious about what my future might hold: Y/N

- I'm tugged by way too many outside forces – people, organizations, or tasks undone that need just a little something more from me: Y/N

- My life has become one of getting it done for others: Y/N

- I have been very satisfied with who I have been in the world: Y/N

- With the changes happening, I feel out of control: Y/N

- I wake up somewhat anxious: Y/N

- I measure my success in my intention throughout the day: Y/N

- At the end of each day, I rank how well I achieved my intentions: Y/N

- I am so joyful during the day, people notice: Y/N

- My energy is sustained throughout the day (I don't feel tired in the afternoon): Y/N

- I'm curious and engage with wonder more than judgment: Y/N

- I courageously ask for the things I want, stepping in, instead of stepping away: Y/N

- I have the conversations I need to have, stepping in, instead of stepping away: Y/N

- Even though my future focus has shifted, I still feel super productive: Y/N

- I am easily distracted (that darn internet, TV, top desk drawer, etc.): Y/N

- It's easy to put other people before myself: Y/N

- I, in fact, do put other people's needs before my own: Y/N

- I don't let other people "in" too closely: Y/N

- I don't want people to know what I'm *really* thinking: Y/N

- I judge myself pretty harshly: Y/N

- I have to admit, I do judge others harshly, too: Y/N

- No one really knows what dreams I have for my future: Y/N

- When I ask, I feel supported: Y/N

- When I *don't* ask, I feel supported: Y/N

- People notice me when I come into a room: Y/N

- People like to be around me (no matter whether extrovert or introvert): Y/N

- I easily share my thoughts: Y/N

- I readily share my opinions: Y/N

- I freely share my feelings: Y/N

- I trust myself: Y/N

- Others trust me: Y/N

Okay, this list could go on for another few pages. Let's pause for a second. Even if you didn't actually take the assessment by writing, be honest with yourself here. What themes of thought came up? You might be feeling pretty sassy right now, thinking "I've got this. I can go boldly into my transition. It's this 'gracefully' part that I'm not sure about." Or you might feel a little set back by your honest assessment, "I am just so unsure in my life right now. I need to get a whole lot clearer before I can feel a whole lot bolder."

You might be feeling something else entirely. You are still in this beautiful space of transition and in the place of creating *your* next chapter of *your* life. Welcoming it leads to grace. Compassion and gratitude lay the foundation for moving forward.

Regrets, you've had a few. And fear, you might have a little.

The ability to move forward gracefully and boldly depends on your ability to let go of both regret and fear. Acknowledgement of where you've been, what you did do in spite of all that you left undone, leads to a sense of completion. Only from there, from the internal assessment of completion of one chapter in your life, can you fully engage in moving forward and creating somewhat limitless dreams for the future.

This is bridge building. This is moving across, making transitions, in the true sense of the word. You carefully, lovingly, gently, and boldly (perhaps somewhat paradoxically) lay to rest just one of the roles you played over the last several decades.

In the next chapter we'll explore further how you to create your identity anew so that you can feel much more solid, present, and engaged. You'll explore what made you the you that you are. And by gaining a greater understanding of who you are and what you value, your transition becomes merely another door to step through. You enter with curiosity and excitement rather than trepidation.

These are the steps to take to move gracefully and boldly into the next great chapter of your life.

You've got this!

Remember to visit www.DynamicTransitions.com/bonus for extra material to support you along your amazing journey!

2

IDENTITY

"But who am I if I'm not a _____? I love what I do!"

That is THE question that my clients blurt out in desperation as they realize that their retirement is imminent, that their family composition is different, or that their days aren't going to be what they used to be: Who Am I If…? *Who am I if* I'm not a dentist? *Who am I if* I'm not a parent to an at-home teenager? *Who am I if* I'm not in a relationship with a partner anymore? *Who am I if* I don't have my old house, job, or other familiar place or things that made me feel so much "at home" ?

We move.

And we move on.

You know your favorite pair of jeans that you finally have to admit you can't really wear anymore? You *have* to let them go! For some people, even separating from their toothbrush is a *little* traumatic.

This transitions stuff is hard. It really is. We humans like predictability. As much as we crave exploring new things to keep our minds stimulated, we like constancy and consistency.

We like to know that if we leave the house one morning, that same house will be there when we come back in the evening. The same is true for our expectations of our jobs, our partners, and our kids. We leave them and expect them to be the same when we return.

The problem is, we don't see the subtle shifts. The ground moves ever so slightly. The grass grows. Our cars weather. Our partners and our kids grow and develop emotionally and physically. And as a result of *their* experiences during the day, they become different. While we might acknowledge that <u>we're</u> different than we were 10 years ago, five years ago, two years ago, last year, last week, or even yesterday, we pretty much expect everything (and everyone) around us to stay much more constant. But they don't. They grow and change, too.

These are the things that come up all the time. It is the reason that this Dynamic Transitions book came to be, and the title is deliberate. A transition is about moving from one state of being to another. You can do that passively. Or, you can make these moves with full engagement and enthusiasm, dynamically!

As we look at "Who am I if..." we will examine the roles and the value of those roles you held in the past. Remember, this book will guide you to move forward gracefully and boldly, so we will look to the future as well. We need to look at "who am I becoming and what does that really mean?"

Referring to the role(s) you hold or held, meaning becomes a major theme of any transition. It is meaning that allows for the graceful movement from one role or status level to another. Besides being anchored by your job, relationship, or some other title or role, there may be questions about who you are and what good you might serve in the world. Those are reasonable questions if now you do not know what to do because what you have always done is no longer available to you. That's going to throw your world a little off. And really, that's the first goal of this book: to get you feeling comfortable being just that bit uncomfortable.

Become comfortably uncomfortable, recognizing that the stream of time continues to flow and that we are each a part of it. Our circumstances shift. And when they do, we can be left feeling a little uncomfortable. What was normal no longer exists.

Sitting in that space of tolerating, or, in fact, welcoming the uncomfortable, takes practice and talent. Yes, it takes talent. And as with any skill, you build it by attending to it. In so doing, you become better, and better, and better.

Again, the first goal here is for you to become comfortably uncomfortable. And, as you remind yourself that of course you can tolerate change — you've done it up to this point and you are now the oldest you have ever been — you ready yourself to embrace the next goal: to feel a little more confident with the direction and opportunities that lie ahead.

Though the existential crisis of "who am I?" is real, the question of "am I what I do?" demands a resounding "NO." You are not defined by any one role.

Go back in time a bit. Think about who you were as a kid. Think about the role you played in your family, and what number child you were: whether an only child, the oldest, the middle, the youngest or somewhere in between in a blended family of some sort. Think about who you were to your friends. Were you the smart one? Were you the clever one? Were you the one that was quick with the joke? Were you the one that "acted out" or maybe provided the best distraction? Were you the "parent" in the family, taking the lead and making sure everyone else had what they needed?

Each of those roles helped to define who you have become. They don't anchor you there. They don't limit who you _can_ become in the future. Certainly, those roles have helped to define you to this point. You were rewarded in some way for being that person, or that kind of person. As the oldest, perhaps you took on more responsibility. As the youngest, perhaps you were cared for or "babied" just a little bit more. In school, your friends rewarded you for being a certain type of person. They relied on you for being that certain type of person, and you felt valued.

Extrinsic rewards (applause, gifts, and other displays of acceptance) lead to reinforced behavior, and your interactive style in the world was shaped. While this is certainly the abbreviated version of how an identity comes into being, if you think about it, every step of the way you were rewarded for becoming who you became, and the transitions that you underwent were secured.

Transitions can also be counted in birthday celebrations. At age 12, your next birthday became one of transitions as you became a teenager. Again, moving from 19 to 20 you left the teens and were stuck in some 'almost' place, not yet 21, eagerly awaiting donning the mantle and title of "full adult." The years that followed also formed you. Whether you continued on to college or began a career (or maybe juggled both), your identity changed again. You were no longer tied to who you were as a school kid. You were no longer under your parents' roof. And you deepened your path to "individualize." Individualization, the way in which a person is distinguished from others, is not done in a vacuum. By definition, you must individualize from some role you were a part of in the past. Growing away from an old role is individualization, and it is done in relationship with, and to, others.

As an aside, we currently see more adults (Gen X, Y, and Z) being the "boomerang kids" who moved out and have returned "home" because they could not find a way to manage in the world on their own. Individualization – moving out of a past role into one of mature adulthood – is stifled as old roles and familiar routines push their way back in. Moving on from old roles takes effort. Again, identity isn't formed in a vacuum. It is the engagement with others that helps to form who we are in this now globally-connected world. And so we push away. You form a new sense of self, of "me," in relationship to who you had been and who you are becoming with others.

Here, the term "others" includes people and the environment. Think about it. You did not fully abandon all that you were. You took some of that with you. Think about the role you brought forward. Whether that was the role of the joyful distracter or perhaps the role of the "brainiac," you brought that role into a new set of friends, teachers, and other authority figures. You learned what worked. You learned what people rewarded you for. You learned what you felt good doing. As you became more of an adult, you figured out what you became good at. You entertained new career ideas, and you got on a path. You met new people. And, perhaps, you even found somebody with whom you could partner. And at that point, your role as an individual became your role to someone else in "couple-hood" or partnership.

Remember that while the past might have gotten you here, it is just that: the past. It neither predicts nor comprises the future unless you take that past with you. And that is a choice. You grow, and your new role is molded.

What does it mean to move from being a child to an independent adult to an adult in a relationship? What does it mean to move from being a couple to slide into becoming parents in what feels like a sudden move? And as you guide a young life, still feeling as a youth yourself, what happens to you as they grow through their stages of development?

Your life changes.

The way you look at life changes.

You now draw from your experience and your perspective as you attempt to guide others through the landmines you encountered on your path.

You have perspective!

And that's where we're heading next. We will be taking an outside view at your past and current roles. Here, we look at what you value. Remember this: PERSPECTIVE IS EVERYTHING. In order to gain a more solid perspective on your direction and to create more positive outcomes for your efforts, it makes sense to take inventory of your current values-based state.

You will also find this assessment available for download at www.DynamicTransitions.com/bonus

Your identity is based on the value you perceive of the difference you make to others. It has been said that we exist to bear witness to others' lives. We do more than that. We not only witness, we shape and are shaped by the experiences we share with others. From those experiences we create a sense of self-worth, and from that we grow our personal identity.

Simple, right?

How do we actually value who we were, who we are, and who we are becoming? The key lies in actually taking some time to reflect. You might sense a small theme here. Most people like to distract themselves with doing. Here, you are being asked to spend some time in that special space of simply being. Do your best to tolerate the thoughts that arise as you begin to explore the inward journey anew.

SELF-ASSESSMENT: Current Identity – Self Worth Is An Inside Job

Personal value develops from so much more than simply what you do or what you have. In fact, your worth may be assessed by evaluating who you are and the difference you make in the lives of others. (For more information on creating value and meaning in your life, see <u>The Significance Factor</u> and <u>the Success and Significance online course</u>.)

For most people, that is exactly why transition is so difficult. Transition may change some of the factors by which have assessed your own value and identity. Personal value and identity develop from so much more than simply what you do or what you have.

Remember *the* question:

Who am I if I'm not a _____?

Begin by looking at the current patterns of interaction you have in the world. Where do you go? With whom do you interact? What do you require to make your day go smoothly? What do you need to make your day more constant/consistent? What do you rely on?

These questions help to explore: What Makes You *YOU*?

Ready? Go!!!

Here you will explore your life and what has anchored your identity in the areas of the people, places, etc., that contribute to the positive feelings you have about who you are –

It will make a difference for you to take some time to reflect on each of these areas. Doing so will allow your transition to the next great stage of your life to flow much more smoothly!

Use a journal, or write in the margins.

Just make sure you take/make notes!

People

A) Parents, step-parents, bonus-parents, etc. – List them separately:
   a. Did you grow up with them?
   b. Did you know <u>their</u> values growing up?
   c. Which of their values do you think you absorbed/ adopted?
   d. Which did you reject?

B) Partner – current or most recent:
   a. What values would you say you share?
   b. How do you contribute most to his/her life?
   c. In what ways does he/she support you in your life?
   d. What *feeling* comes up when you think about him/her?
   • This could be positive or not-so-positive; your honesty with yourself here is hugely important.

C) Children – no matter their ages, because even adult kids are still "kids." Even if they have since passed, still list them here. Each has had an impact on who you are. List them separately:
   a. How old is each child in your life (include grandkids if you have any that you see/influence somewhat regularly)
   b. What word or phrase describes your influence with them? (e.g., play, guide, teach, role-model, ignore, contain, punish, etc.) Put that phrase next to each on your list.
   c. For each child you listed, how do you think they see you? List a word or phrase that they might use to describe your engagement with them. List a word or phrase that describes your impact upon them.

It is important to take some time with this. Do not attempt to rush this process. You are at the first part of this, and you need to acknowledge what impact each of your children had, and has, on you. This is HUGE in gaining a broader perspective of who you are and allowing yourself to move gracefully AND boldly into the next great phase of your life.

D) Other Family Members –
   a. List those with whom you have regular contact.
   b. List those whom you seldom see, but hold in a particular role in your life.

E) Team – Like family, team members hold a particular role with you, and you with them. What role do your team members play in your life?
   a. List the members of your team and the role they hold or held for you.

F) Vendors & Contractors – Yes, those outside people who show up regularly and with whom you still have a relationship of some kind. Who are they? For some they are like extended family members. While you may see them infrequently, they impact your life. List them here –

G) Other People – There are people whom you see or interact with that impact who you are. It could be the host at your favorite restaurant, or your coffee barista, who greets you by name. It could be the other mom in the park with whom you are not really acquainted, but you connect at that level for that brief time. Who else?

Places

The context of the familiar – This is another big one. On a personal note, I grew up in the house that my dad (who is 96 years old at the time of this book's first publication) still owns and lives in. When I visit, I could climb the steps, put my key in the door and navigate that house with my eyes closed. It is familiar. I will miss it when I can no longer return there. And yet, it is not my home. Again, take some time with this category of Places and what is familiar.

A) The road to work/home/etc. – Here, explore the home you have, the home you grew up in if it is still familiar to you, the road you take to work, and anything else that you could pretty much just navigate automatically without much thought. Give it some thought. What makes it familiar? The layout or route? The sights? The smells?

List the places and the associated things that make them familiar.

   a. The restaurants you used to frequent – what about them made them familiar or contributed to your role or identity? Were there favorite foods, smells, sights, sounds, or even things you'd touch?

   b. The other shops – you passed or frequented certain shops. It's possible it was a whole shopping area, a main street or a mall. What made that part of who you are? That is, when you think of that area, what tugs at your core identity?

   c. The view from *that* place – Any particular place that you have found your thoughts drifting to – what did you see from the outside? What did you see from the inside?

    d. The smell, sounds, and touch/feel (including breeze, fog, etc.) – All of it – the sensations that go with the place you are drawn back to – what comes to mind as you reflect back?

Things

It could be a vase, a picture, or an old broken stereo. It could even be a potato peeler. What things fed your identity from the past to the current?
a) At home
b) At work
c) Out and about

Clothing

Did you dress a particular way? How did that serve your identity?
A) Uniform
B) Smock
C) Coat
D) Casual or Biz

Instruments – The things you use(d) in your daily life

A) Car
B) Technical tools
C) Pens
D) Computer
E) TV
F) Cookware
G) Etc.

Financial – What did you do for and with money? How did that shape your identity?

A) Income
B) Expenses –where did you spend your money that helped you form your identity? (this isn't a balance sheet)
   a. Travel
      i.   Local, around town
      ii. Cross country
      iii. Beyond

   b. Food
      i.   Grocery Stores
      ii. Coffee Shops
      iii. Restaurants

   c. Outings – where did you go for fun?

Social/Recreational – List what you did for fun that helped shape who you are. Sure, you could have hung out at the local pizza place or gone bowling with friends. Maybe you went to concerts or to the movies. What kinds of things did you do and with whom?

A) Places
B) People

Health +/- – For better or worse, the role(s) we have had affect our health and vice versa. We could be in great health and have become a cross-country or marathon runner, or in poor health and become a shut in. Think about the things you engaged in that affected your health for better or worse.

A) What have been the effects of doing that?
- a) Most have both positive and not-so-positive effects on health
  - a. Posture
  - b. Allergens
  - c. Noise – high Dbs
  - d. Other – just jot down what comes to mind when you think about your health and your identity.

Wasn't that amazing? Seriously, if you took your time with that inventory, you ended up going down a memory lane that allowed you to make leaps from where you were to where you are. That is exceptionally important as you glide gracefully and boldly across into the land of where you are headed.

So, good for you!

We have a little more role definition ahead. It's easier from here. As with anything, getting the foundational "stuff" behind you creates the pad from which to leap. You have done some great work in this chapter. You identified a lot of the things that serve to create and support your current identity. Good for you.

The next chapter explores what it all means. Hugely important in your development are the values you hold. There are core values and situational values. Take a breath, then turn the page. Here we go!

3

VALUES

In psychology, It was historically thought that your personality was essentially set by the time you were six years old. So much has changed since those early theories were developed. Advances in neuroplasticity research has dovetailed over into the psychological arena. Not only can neural pathways be rerouted, but the mysterious thing called personality can change over time, as well.

The ability to change over time is also true of identity. The people, places, and things to which we attach our identity change. Our emotional attachment to people, places, and things in our past also morphs. And accompanying, or perhaps underlying, those changes in both personality and identity is the variances in values. As a six-year-old, a child might treasure treats such as ice cream. As an adult, that child might grow to treasure reward such as a salary. But that falls down the ladder of importance when that adult has a family, which now becomes the main object of importance. The six-year-old might not have treasured the familial connection that the now 30-something does. Yes, love of family was probably there for the child, but the active _value_ of connection may or may not have been.

A parent's shift in focus from self to family connection is but one obvious value that changes. From sweet treats and other forms of reward to family connection. DynamicLeader® coaching clients who are in their late forties and fifties report that the pursuit of money is less urgent. In fact, the value of introspection rises higher on their list of priorities. The value of connection to family and to God is frequently included on this list.

What changes and how? First of all, we no longer live in small villages where everyone knows everyone else, and the way a person is becomes the way that person will always be. We live in a more global community now. The Internet connects us to new cultures, and air travel now makes it easy to visit those cultures in person. Whether we travel or not, we are instantly affected by ideas from around the globe. Politically, socially, economically, and even spiritually, we are introduced to concepts and ideas that spark the imagination and provoke a shift in both values and identity.

Think about some of your values that have changed over time. As a student in high school you may have valued social connection over good grades. If you went on to college, you may have valued study and managed to balance social connection secondarily. Or, for some, it was the other way around. The value of study was overridden by the new-found freedom to explore new social connections. Chances are you have at least observed both ends of this spectrum.

What other values have changed over time? For the young entrepreneur, profit at all costs often becomes the battle cry. For the more seasoned entrepreneur, balance is what is sought most often. Just about every person caught up in the fast-paced hustle of a demanding career dreams of their vacation, count-ing the days until their escape. Have you ever pushed to get things done to go on vacation, spending a week in a relaxed environment, only to question _why_ you should actually return to that lifestyle you left?

Yeah. That. Our values change. We get glued onto the con-veyer-belt of all of that "should-do" stuff. Think about what you have done because you were "supposed to." Did you study, go to college, get a job, or help out a family relative who needed you? Did you go out on your own, find a partner, settle down, and start a family including pets and some form of SUV or mini-van?

Do you follow recipes that pop up on your favorite social media platform or enjoy the fantasy drama that unfolds on streaming TV? Before the summer of 1991, none of that existed. Does that blow your mind? Only in the past few decades has our world truly expanded. And it has been only in the last decade that we have seen amazing coordinated research in the neurosciences, including research in neuroplasticity and neuropsychology.

What does that mean to you? It means that you have grown and changed with the influences that have flooded you from outside of your tiny village. You drive to work in another town, working with people who also come from other towns. You receive text messages from family, friends, and colleagues from around the world. You watch videos created in other parts of the world. Then you might "like" and "share" these to still more people. Does any of that affect your identity? You bet it does! You are influenced and influencing those beyond the curtain of your immediate surroundings.

Can you agree that you have changed a few of the things that you value? And might you also agree that the people, places, and things to which you were emotionally tethered for your identity have changed too?

Since values and identity are not as stuck or structured as we once believed, we will need to grab a snapshot in time of your current roles and the values you ascribe to each. As with the last chapter, you will need your journal. You could use the margins of this book, though it might just get a little crowded. You will find you get more out of the next section by actually actively engaging in it.

Each of us plays multiple roles, and our identity is tied securely to at least one of them. In the last chapter, you examined your historical development a bit. The purpose of this next exercise is to break out the various roles you play currently. Then, perhaps most important, is the examination of your personal values associated with each of those roles.

In terms of your-_self_, your most personal inner self, what role do you see yourself playing in the world? When you are alone at night, how do you think of yourself? When you come bounding out the door in the morning (perhaps it is when you are fresh out of the shower or have just had your first sip of coffee), how do you feel about yourself?

Take a moment here. List the various roles you play (superhero, fix-it guy/gal, moneymaker, laid-back dude/dudette, or …?).

Roles of the **Self:**
A)
B)
C)
D)
E)
F)

You might have more than six. Most people have at least three that spring to mind right away. Once you've captured your roles, it is important for you to then spend a moment to think about and identify the values that are associated with each. There could be multiple values for each role listed.

For example, if you selected teacher and breadwinner as two roles you play, you might then list the associated values of patience, knowledge, learning, creativity, and creative expression for the role of teacher (which could be one role you play as a parent). For the role of breadwinner, you might come up with values such as financial stability, providing for family and future, etc.

Notice that you are not given a selection of values from which to pull. You get to create them, or at least name them. What is it you value about each role? Another way to ask that is, what drives you? What makes you want to keep the role you have?

From above:

Roles: ———————————————————— **Values:**

A)

B)

C)

D)

E)

F)

Here, let your mind loose as you create a list of values for each of the roles you identified for your *Self*, above.

And in your family, what roles do you play? Your current family – not necessarily your immediate family. When you think "family," what comes to mind? Rather, *who* comes to mind?

And as you think about that person or persons, what role do you play in their lives? Who are you to them? You need not list the people here; simply list the roles that come to mind as you think about Family.

Then, to expedite the process, also list the values that are associated with each of the roles.

Do that here for **Family**:

Roles: ———————————————————— **Values:**

   A)

   B)

   C)

   D)

   E)

   F)

Let it get messy. Whether you are using this book to capture your notes or using your own journal, let it get messy. Unless, of course, organization and tidiness are core values. Then just keep it neat.

Okay, so you now have two key areas behind you. There are a few more to go here. These exercises should serve to inspire, as you glean new insights by reflecting inward a bit. Keep going! This work is foundational to your graceful and bold transition.

Socially, you have various roles. You are the friend, confidant, or drinking buddy. You are the best party thrower. Or you are the wallflower and homebody — social is not a "thing" for you, so socially you are isolated.

There are no wrong or right answers. Simply list what comes to mind for you. Spend some time here, not a lot, but some. Then, think about the attributes and values associated with each social role you've listed, and add those.

Social:

Roles: —————————————————————— **Values:**

A)
B)
C)
D)
E)
F)

As you notice yourself owning your current world, you might be getting hints as to how you will boldly and gracefully take on your new role(s) in the world. Yep! This is going to be fun. And you are going to be powerful making this next move.

Now the stage is set for what is coming next. You have three more short exercises to go through. You're getting the hang of this and doing great. Give these next lists the same thought (or even more thought) than you gave to the first few.

The next area, that of Finance, might be a little tougher to conquer. What role might you play around money? You may only have one or two roles with this category. This one demands you look at your relationship with money. Do you welcome it? Are you secretly afraid of it? Are you confused by it? Volumes have been written about this. If you have not yet paid attention to this category directly, it is past time. If you have, congratulations! Either way, take a moment to list your role(s) and the accompanying values for each role listed.

Financial:

Roles: ———————————————————**Values:**

    A)

    B)

    C)

    D)

    E)

    F)

Your identity is often connected to what you do for a living. These questions now focus on your career or work life. Think about the title that you have. Of course, you know that you are not that title. What roles – plural – do you play here? You are surely a support to some and perhaps a leader to others. Are you a confidant or a commandant?

Ready?

Go!!!

Professional/Career:

Roles: ———————————————————**Values:**

    A)

    B)

    C)

    D)

    E)

    F)

Often missed are these next, and last, two. You play a role with your *Self* in a different way than earlier identified. Think about your body. What role does the physical you have with your identity? For some, the aches and pains that come with being a bit older affect the way they think about the world. For others, pain is just a motivator to do more, or to change.

You have this! What role does your physical body play with your identity?

Physical:

Roles: ——————————————————————— **Values:**

   A)

   B)

   C)

   D)

   E)

   F)

Last on the list for you to explore is that of the Spiritual. For some reading this, there is a strong connection to something beyond themselves. That is an easy one. For others, it is just as easy, but the labels are different. Surprisingly, the values show some overlap here. And, because you are not comparing yourself to anyone else (part of transitioning both gracefully and boldly is to do it as yourself, for yourself), look only at your own relationship to Spirit or connection beyond yourself to nature, other people, etc.

On the next page, put specific words to a connection that is rarely clearly defined!

(Spiritual) Connection Beyond Self:

Roles: ──────────────────────────────── **Values:**

A)

B)

C)

D)

E)

F)

While this last category is the trickiest to write about, it is likely not that difficult for you as the reader to get through. You have a specific connection and you have values that attach to that connection. Whether a scientifically-based atheist, a faith-based religious devotee, or somewhere in between, certain values are linked to your beliefs. From these values, your identity becomes clearer.

Now what? Now you get to choose what is working for you and what might be an old role or belief that you are ready to shift a little.

On the next page, you will find some questions for reflection – Questions to provoke some thoughts to take with you through the rest of this book:

• What themes emerged?

• Was this easy or somewhat difficult for you?

• Which sections were the easiest?

• Why do you think that might be?

- Which parts were the most difficult and what made them so difficult?

- Which of the roles or the values are you the proudest of?

- Which are you least proud of?

- Which values might need some work?

- Which values have endured the longest in your own personal history?

- Which values will you be taking with you into the next great phase of your life?

4

ACKNOWLEDGING THE SHIFT

You have done some great work thus far to define your identity and the things that matter to you by diving deeply into your values and role definition. This is tough stuff, which some people only accomplish over the course of many years. Unfortunately for those taking that timeline, by the time they have defined who they were, they have changed. You have taken a masterful shortcut. But if you decided to take a not-so-masterful shortcut by skipping any of the previous exercises, you are now strongly encouraged to go back and complete them. Theory comes to life when you make the process yours.

It is important here to look at what has changed in your life. Explore what is different for you today than from a few years back. The world was quite different not that long ago, from politics to hairstyles. Things are not what they were. And you are not who you were.

Every moment, in so many ways, everything changes. Everything. Even as you read this, not only have you changed, but so too has the medium on which you are reading this. Whether paper or digital, it is changing right now! Weird, isn't it? Sure, it might be odd or uncomfortable to think about all of the bio-chemical shifts occurring every moment of every day. Yet, if you extrapolate that thinking, it makes it easier to recognize something important.

The shift is happening with or without your approval.

You are in relationship with the world and with each of the roles you identified in the previous chapter. As wonderful as that is, and it is, you might need to recognize something that is both elementary and profound. It is about that relationship thing. It is not static.

That is, any relationship, whether with your partner, your kids, your office mates, or that two-day-old pizza in the fridge, it is not just on hold. The nature of relationships can be found in the Latin roots of the word itself.

Re-Lation-Ship

Here, *Ship* is the state of something (like a township or fellowship).

Lation is about movement (surprise!) or the way things come together (like celestial bodies moving around each other or gears coming together).

And *Re* is the easy part of this. If you were to re-do something, you would be doing it again, right?

Putting that all together, you have the state of moving or coming together *again*. This means that your relationships at home, at work, and in the world are in motion all the time. They are either growing or degenerating, depending on where you put your energy. (And if you have teenagers, you might not be sure from moment to moment where you stand on this one.)

This also means that the nature of the relationship you have with yourself is not static. Your understanding of *Self* grows or degenerates depending on the energy you give that relationship, too. While some choose to passively ignore who they are in the world, you have chosen a different path. Congratulations!

Think about something that has withstood the test of time. What? The great pyramids? The U.S. Constitution? That Christmas fruitcake you were given? There are many objects and principles that are time-tested. And do they really withstand the test of time? The pyramids have eroded. The U.S. Constitution has been challenged and amended. Everything changes over time. Well, except maybe that fruitcake.

You will see the phrase "...what this means is..." multiple times in this book. It is important to glean the meaning from every concept presented. By doing so, you get to choose what to take with you and how to move forward in your life.

And that is what this means – you ARE moving forward in your life. It becomes essential to acknowledge the shift, your shift, from who you were to who you are. From here, you can then begin to build the bridge to who you are becoming.

Dynamic Transitions are about becoming by design.

Becoming by design? Becoming what? Becoming who? Becoming *the* what and *the* who *HOW?* Design starts with choice and we will dive into that shortly. Seeds are planted here for you to begin thinking about the becoming by design concept.

Who you are becoming comes down to how you choose to handle your relationship(s) to yourself, to others, and to your environment. Ultimately this comes down to you looking at the fact that you are in relationship with the world around you and beyond. Given that you are in relationship, you are in motion. There is a flow. And right now, that flow is getting your attention.

Remember that you are here to *move gracefully and boldly* into the next great chapter of your life. That graceful part means that you are recognizing and acknowledging that a shift is happening, whether the transition you are in is a major one for you or a slight shift in the way you engage in your day (from diet and exercise to social engagement and sleep cycles).

As you would gracefully welcome someone to a party, whether you genuinely like that person or not, you acknowledge them and welcome them. Here, you acknowledge that a shift is happening. You might wonder, as you would wonder with a slightly unpredictable party guest, what is going to happen next. Since things are no longer as they were, you actually have some say in that.

For now, as we move forward, you acknowledge that the party guest is here. That shift IS happening in your life. It isn't necessarily fun, but it might be. So really, why don't you see what kind of mischief you and that guest can get into!

Ah, now by acknowledging that you are in the process of shift, of moving across, truly in relationship and coming together with your *Self* again, you can open yourself to new possibilities. By welcoming the change that is ahead, you gain grace. And perhaps that also has a capital at the beginning, Grace.

By welcoming the change, you gain Grace.

And as you do so, you practice being in that space. You become, literally, graceful... that is, Grace-full.

And with all of that, there may still be internal struggle. How do you know when you are through that? How can you move gracefully into a relationship when you are not quite done letting go? You have acknowledged that you are IN the shift. You know that you can be graceful, but right now might feel like you have a foot in both worlds of grace and clumsiness.

That feeling of "not quite right" is still normal. It is. You understand grace the way you understand how watching people dancing on television means that smoothness is possible. It may not be in you right now. You may not fully own it.

What steps must you go through to get there? Why does this have to be so hard? Why can't things go back to the way they were? Yes, these are all great questions. And they can be answered as you turn the page.

What a wonderful journey you are on. Transitions, like a party guest you may not be too sure about, flow more smoothly when you acknowledge them. And now it is time to step boldly into a broader understanding of this process. Where did all of those questions come from? Here, you go, boldly and gracefully...

5

LETTING GO

Acknowledging that your situation has truly changed, that you actually *are in the shift,* is a brand-new beginning for you. In fact, it's an essential first step. Because we are so bound by what we had, and our so identity tied to who we were, it really is essential to acknowledge that shift.

In 1969, Elizabeth Kübler-Ross established the first ground breaking framework for observing the five distinct mental and emotional stages which a person undergoes during the grieving process following a loss. Her studies were primarily centered on death and dying, and for the most part, targeted the emotions one experiences following the loss of a loved one. Since then, her work has been extrapolated and expounded upon; the same stages of grief can be seen in individuals diagnosed with a severe (typically terminal) disease. However, the grief and loss stages may also be applied to the emotional states that accompany the loss of <u>anything</u> that is particularly special to an individual, such as a job, a spouse, or a beloved pet,

While taking some minor liberties with the grief and loss framework, we can apply these five stages of loss to the work of Dynamic Transitions. Notably, we shall stay attentive to how to best move boldly and gracefully into the next great chapter of your life.

You may grieve the loss of anything, from car keys to a significant other. The extent to which you are affected varies and really is not predictable.

Your job is just to notice.

THE GRIEF AND LOSS STAGES

You may have heard about these stages, or you may be quite familiar with them, In which case this will serve as a reminder. Or, perhaps this concept and framework are brand new to you. Let the following guide you along your own Dynamic Transition!

Stage One. Denial

It is not unusual to want to cling to the known. In actuality, it is quite normal to seek constancy and consistency in your life. We humans like that. In fact, we need that. When a transition happens, we do what we can psychologically to prove to ourselves that the change/shift/transition we are facing just isn't so.

In a sudden transition, such as the loss of a loved one, we look for places that we had seen that loved one, we review texts, and we anticipate the phone ringing as it always had. We search for the familiar, hoping to reassure ourselves that what was still is.

In a career-path shift or some other life change, it is not unusual to search for the familiar. Here again, we do what we can psychologically to prove to ourselves that what was, might still be available to us.

The work you did on your values in the previous chapters will become very essential at this stage. Who you were doesn't have to change. Who you were doesn't have to be molded into something that does not include your essential core-values. In the last chapter you did some great work defining your past Identities and to acknowledge that a shift might actually be happening. In so doing, you laid the groundwork to move from denial into the next few stages of letting go.

Stage Two. Anger

In working through the grief and loss stages, it is not unusual to be flat-out angry at pretty much anything. You are letting go of your past identity and engaging in an accounting of what was. And therefore, being a little angry at this point — at yourself, at circumstances, even at God for having put you in this position — feels like a normal response. You have so many questions that no one can answer!

How much time have you spent, invested, or wasted? And if you consider it an investment, what did it yield? We begin this journey of life, and we climb this mountain at the top of which we think we will find success. When we get there, we find that what was *supposed to be* success is not quite as fulfilling as we first anticipated, but here we are.

So, we lay out our picnic blanket and stay awhile.

We explore, we build a house, we build a business, and we enjoy it. In fact, it's the process of all that building that helps to develop our identity.

But there is more.

We look at what we've built. We're proud of it, and yet, we ache for more. We invest further. We develop relationships. We become a part of the community or communities, both locally and perhaps more globally.

We invest and we serve and we develop a stronger and stronger sense of who we are, forging our identity.

And then it shifts. What *was* has become no longer what *is*, and the battle cry of "who am I if I'm not a _____?" becomes an impassioned plea to develop a new identity.

This is a major step forward, though the internal battle is tough. Here you move from Stage One of denial, where you might say to yourself, "Oh no, I still am that," into Stage Two where you desperately attempt to cling to what was, and at the same time recognize that *what was* is no more.

At this point you might begin to wonder whether it was all worth it. You ask the question, "Is this all there is?" As things shift so dramatically, you look at what you are left with, and you wonder about your return on investment of time, money, energy.

It is the time you can't get back. You can renew your energy, and you can renew your money, but the investment of time has passed. You ask, "Was it worth it?"

It is there that the passing of one chapter in your life creates a sense of loss. Anger (in Stage Two) comes from feeling as though some outside source took that precious part of your life from you. Like a treasured antique or family heirloom destroyed in a fire, are the memories enough? At your very core, your identity is threatened. You no longer have what you had. You no longer are who you were. Of course you are angry.

Your team, your family, your friends, and even strangers (for example, the cashier at the supermarket or the waitstaff at a restaurant) may sense a general grumpiness about you. Anger doesn't have to be expressed by yelling. Anger is sometimes seen as a general displeasure with the basics of life.

It's possible that you find yourself pushing away from those that you love, even if they are the ones that are the most familiar. They have created at least part of the context for your identity, and yet because there is a loss in one area of your life, you find yourself pushing away and isolating. In doing so, perhaps you are also taking inventory of what these pieces of your life actually mean.

This is a difficult phase. You may find yourself evaluating everything about your investment of energy, money, and time. (Here, your energy refers to your investment of personal giving of self. This then includes the investment of yourself into your relationships, as well.)

Your investments In these areas may be similar to how some people have played the stock market. They invest little bits here and there, and they play for the "long term." They plan for the future based on an uncertain past. They ride the bubble. They endure the burst. And when it's time to withdraw, there is hope that their investments will have yielded something of value. Sometimes the payoff is there and sometimes not, and as you look at the yield of all of your investments of energy, money, and time, as this life-chapter comes to a close, anger begins to dovetail over into the next stage of grieving.

That stage is called Bargaining.

Stage Three: Bargaining

It's possible that you found yourself saying, "If only..." or, "What if I....?" If you were asking those questions as you were reflecting back, then you were probably firmly in the stage called bargaining. The concept here is similar to that part of the grieving process when either an individual or their family member has been diagnosed with a terminal disease. You might see bargaining show up as negotiation about the potential future behavior. "If only I could be healthy, I would change my lifestyle." This is not an unusual statement to be made in this stage. That statement is made to themselves, to God, or to anyone who will listen. Sometimes these types of statements are made looking back in remorse, "If only I had ...." For you, as you transition from your current job or relationship or life status, it is important to look at the things you were holding onto and what you were bargaining for.

For example, I work with many dentists who, at the end of their career, will say things like, "Well, maybe I could just keep working one or two days a week or even maybe just one or two days a month." They tell me that they want to keep doing dentistry until they're 70 – or even 80 – years old. Those are certainly firm bargaining statements and land you smack-dab in the middle of the grief and loss process. A better statement that would have offset this would have been made perhaps two to five years ago along the lines of, "I have, in my plan, to sell to an associate and maintain my position for one day a week for the six months following the sale." The key here is PLAN. We shall explore how that concept plays into your bold and graceful Dynamic Transition shortly.

As you go through a potential bargaining stage, take a look at the things you were reluctant to let go of. In relationships, are you keeping old photos around? Are you keeping that old voicemail message? If you are in the midst of a house move, are you holding on to those things you uncovered that you had put away for "some day?"

To give you clues about your own process, the questions that are telltale signs that you are firmly in bargaining include:

- I wonder if I could …

- If only I could …

- Maybe I can …

- Maybe he/she will …

Each of these is hopeful and, *hope is essential during grieving.*

You need to know, or at least feel, that there is a better tomorrow. And really, that is what hope is all about. Tomorrow will be better. It is important to be optimistic about your future. It is also important to be somewhat "realistic" as well.

That is, to realize and to acknowledge outwardly that the old thing — the job, the relationship, the location, the situation that is now in the past—will not be brought with you with you and that, then, leads to the next phase in the grieving process.

Stage Four: Depression

Bargaining gives way to a sense of feeling blue. The real loss is actually experienced at this point in the grieving process, and a mild depression sets in. There is an unease or an unhappiness that comes in life at this point. It feels like nothing will make you happy. You wonder if you'll ever be as happy as you were before. In this case, depression can last what seems like a few moments or can carry on for several years. It is common for it to last several weeks.

Depression is an essential part of the grieving process because it is from this place that a new identity is formed.

Unlike anger, where a return on investment has been evaluated, during depression one evaluates one's own personal values. As you trudge through the futile and fatalistic land of emotional quicksand, you ask, "What's next?" "What is worthy of the next investment?" "Is anything worth it, really?"

Remember that work you did early on in examining your values and what role you played? There is a reason that you went through that exercise. In the grieving stage of depression, you are in a place of deep self-reflection. Everything seems gray and perhaps a little muddled. Deep down you know that it will work out, but the hole in your heart feels real.

Personal loss—whether of the status in a relationship, the death of a loved one, moving from a house where you enjoyed not only the home but the community, and the changing of a career —all seem like they will never be the same again. The truth is, they never *will* be the same again. All you are left to do, then, is honor that space or hole created in your heart, filling it with positive memories.

It is this that creates the bridge to the final stage in the grieving process: Acceptance.

Stage Five: Acceptance

Having laid the foundation for building memories and holding on to them as well, you are now able to maintain something that is valuable from here forward: perspective! You now have a backward-looking view at *what was,* allowing you a forward-looking view to what could be. Acceptance is the stage wherein the healing happens. You begin to feel as though the memories will sustain you, and you begin to create a new identity and a new life.

You look forward with a renewed hope and, sure, you might be a little bit wistful about what the past held. You might look back on your memories fondly. Either way, doing so serves to create the foundation for what's possible because now you look forward. In the past during this grieving process, you have gone through two "negative" stages: anger and depression. Accepting the reality that you have shifted from what was creates a space for you to build something new. Acceptance is usually a very calm place. And in that calmness comes clarity. We will explore the concept of clarity a little bit later (a few chapters from now).

Now, recognizing that you have let go, you begin to hold a clearer head and heart space about the possibilities for your future.

In the phase of acceptance, you take the first steps into planning for the future. Though tentative, you yield to the emptiness of the past and look ahead to a place that has begun to look a little brighter. You draw on your core strengths, and you bring with you your core values. You begin to see the value of investing of yourself anew, and in so doing, you create a strong meaning for the new life ahead.

Dynamic Transitions are about the meaning you bring from one phase or chapter of your life into the next. It is by bringing meaning with you that you move boldly AND gracefully into that next great space.

Your life is beginning anew. What will you bring to it?

Some people do not find themselves stressed or living in grief at all. In fact, they feel at peace knowing that where they are heading is going to be great. How does that happen? It is possible that they have done what is known as pre-grieving, or engaged in anticipatory grief.

By getting the grieving "out of the way," you can actually make your transition with grace and aplomb! But the psychology of letting go — the stages you go through to accomplish that — are oh, so similar.

We dive into exploring that next.

As a gift and to help you in your studies, you can find a framework summary of the stages of grieving on your bonus page: www.WaynePernell.com/bonus

6

ANTICIPATORY GRIEF

It might seem odd to put a chapter on loss and grieving *before* a chapter on anticipating that loss and its accompanying grief. However, the previous chapter laid a foundation for your understanding of the flow of the stages. In this section, we focus on the concept of grieving *before* the actual movement, shift or loss. The notion that one can grieve a loss before the actual loss occurs is quite profound and, in actuality, doing so creates a smoother transition at the time of the actual shift.

Pre-Grieving The Loss Makes The Transition Smoother

Just as parents-to-be often prepare a baby's room and engage in what is known as "nesting," parents of college-bound teenagers, for example, end up preparing for empty-nesting by becoming heavily involved in exploring what the potential colleges have to offer and what the rooming or housing situation might be. In

preparing the now-adult-child for leaving the "nest," the grieving phase of Denial is actually shortened quite substantially.
The reality of the shift is simply marked on a calendar.

The transition that has been pre-grieved is still not pain free.
Moms will still feel a tug at their hearts when their "babies" go
off to college.

Similarly, those leaving a career of 30 years or more,
who recognize that the end of their working days is coming,
often mark their departure months, or potentially years, out.
What is helpful in both cases of the child leaving the home
and the career coming to a close is a definitive date. By denot-
ing a specific transition date, it no longer becomes a matter
of "someday" which can be put off indefinitely. The nebulous
"someday" lengthens the potential for grief, and various phases
may be circled back to as a result. By setting a clear date for
departure, the "someday" becomes "this day."

Oftentimes the reason that the passing of an individual
becomes harder for those who are left behind is that the passing was either sudden and/or unexpected, or anticipated as
sometime much later in the future. The "someday" factor plays
a big role here.

Remember that this is all about letting go. You are leaving
behind an identity that you had taken years, perhaps decades,
to build. Your role was special to you, and as that role changes
and evolves into something new, the shift is difficult. Here, with
the date of transition clearly defined, the Denial phase is substantially minimized, both in duration as well as magnitude (the
energy put into the actions surrounding denial).

The second phase of the grieving process, Anger, is also
foreshortened through the anticipatory grieving process. When
it does erupt, however, it is often in the psychological defense
of the individual from feeling pushed out of the tribe. The

not-so-logical self-talk is this: "As I leave, if I find reasons to be mad at you first, then if you are mad at me for leaving, you are just mad that I'm mad."

Essentially, by declaring you are leaving, you will no longer be "one of the cool kids." To understand this from another angle, essentially the concept is that during anticipatory grief, knowing that a change is coming, you might prepare for leaving by being angry about the past, to help yourself mentally justify the change. You might end up undercutting or undermining your previous connections (and those "cool kids" weren't so cool after all, were they? That is, while you might have had some affinity for your past workmates, you may now wonder what you ever saw in them). While not rational, you may simply seek reasons to validate your decision to leave.

Remember that having picked a date, it becomes easier to acknowledge that the shift in position or status is coming. Then, as a means of psychological defense, you might begin finding fault with other people, their habits, or the way that the business operates. It is a way for you to separate from "Them" before they push you out. You begin to regain a feeling of control and give yourself reasons to leave, rather than feel like you will be rejected because you have announced your shift or transition.

The funny thing is that this becomes self-fulfilling. What happens is that by being angry, other people _do_ choose to push you away. The nature of their engagement with you *does* change, and you do end up feeling less connected. The danger is that this cycle will continue, and you will spiral out of control into such an angry state that you are, in fact, either pushed out or you "choose" to remove yourself early. This is noted here so that you can be alert and aware of such a possibility. Bringing it into consciousness gives you greater choices. In terms of Dynamic Transitions, while this behavior in such a transition might be bold, this is hardly graceful.

When in the space of anticipating the transition, the anticipatory grief process is different during the stage of Bargaining than during actual grieving *during* a loss. The biggest key to bargaining here is a focus on (or desire for) the extension of the date of transition. That is, you might find yourself wanting to stay on just that bit more, and just that bit more. You watch the calendar pages turn, knowing that date is going to show up. You begin to wonder whether you couldn't just move it back a bit.

When you anticipate leaving something substantial behind, you actually make room to be able to do that. Your psyche says, "Okay, it's time." Whether that is an old pair of jeans, a specific habit (for example, cutting out sugar), a change in relationship, or transitioning from a career, you ready yourself to let go.

If you find yourself saying, "Just one more ...," then you are firmly in bargaining. Even though you may be in the anticipatory grieving state, you're still bargaining. It's okay, going through the grieving process is actually healthy. The trick is to not hurt yourself while doing it. Don't stay stuck. Keep moving.

Keep moving does NOT mean, "maybe I can take on a different role here." Sure, some people successfully negotiate becoming outside advisors. If the role changes but the organization is the same, you are not in bargaining unless you pine for your old job back. "Yes... sigh... that used to be my desk." Or, worse yet, slipping from bargaining back into anger, "when I worked in that position, we did things <u>this</u> way."

Fluidly moving between stages and back is not uncommon. In this last example, you might be straddling Anger and Bargaining, awaiting the slide into the fourth stage, Depression.

Depression happens when the reality of what was feels as though it were yanked from you somehow. Where the phase of

Anger has energy, Depression looks like withdrawal. You might find yourself isolating from others just a bit more. You no longer participate in the company celebrations. There is a sense of, "why bother."

Unfortunately, if an angry phase was foreshortened in any way, the withdrawal could actually be lengthened. Depression is not just a personal withdrawal but an energetic withdrawal from an outward expression of engagement with people, places or situations. There is a sense of anhedonia (the inability to feel pleasure) and a general malaise that takes over, like a persistent fog that has blown in. The world looks gray and feels like it always will be.

You are letting go of the past while honoring the memories of that past.

The key to keep in mind here is that you really are letting go of the past while holding on to the best memories from that past. You can acknowledge that your investment in that past has been worthwhile, and you can acknowledge that while your status or relationship with your current position is shifting, all of those things that made it worthwhile in the past can be remembered fondly.

By doing this work now, it is akin to releasing pressure that has been building. When you tap the top of a can or bottle of a fizzy drink (soda, sparkling water or champagne), the bubbles come to the top. That is supposed to help the pressure release a little, but it's all still IN the can. So you open the drink very carefully and you hear, "pfffffffffffttttttt." (C'mon, how would you spell that sound?) What happens is that the pressure is released, and you can safely pour your drink. Sometimes, though, it still sprays just a little.

This analogy is meant to say that what you are going through now does not mean that it won't be messy later. It might. You might "get some on you." You might still feel a little lost, and therefore a little angry or depressed.

Feeling lost can give way to fear which can also be the pathway for anger or depression. Even the kindest, calmest animal, when afraid, will lash out. When lashing out and simply being afraid or lost doesn't serve the animal, it simply yields and takes the "punishment" that awaits it. Here, the reference goes to studies in Learned Helplessness.

Going through some of the feelings of loss before the actual event helps to offset or reduce the intensity of the feelings. Will they still exist? Will you still feel something when the time comes? Yes, probably. And when they do, you have a frame of reference for them. Having a date of transition (retirement, relocating, etc.) gives your psyche a target. And you can (and likely will) engage in pre-grieving.

Reflect back on the work you did in identifying your roles and the accompanying values with each role. You looked at the people, places and things that were significant for you. Those are now the things that memories become made of: Your favorite coffee shop where they knew you by name, the smell of the break area at your work, the lighting that never seemed quite right... all of it.

Allow it in.

Acknowledge it.

And release it.

It is not now as it was. It is for someone else to step into and make theirs. It is your gift to the future to release what you held. And it really is okay to stay engaged while you are still IN the place that you will be moving on from. Acknowledge those who you might be leaving behind, and instead of anger, seek gratitude. Living in that space of being grateful for what you had and what you have, allows you to let go with a little more grace. By considering your transition a gift to someone else, you also allow the future to change what you had. You can then look back without resentment.

Anger, Bargaining, and Depression can each be ways that we use to punish ourselves. We are leaving a condition that was well known and causing turmoil in our lives. Even if someone or something did that *to* us. This is an opportunity to step in with forgiveness not only of others, but of yourself. You are, essentially, forgiving yourself for the upset that you are causing yourself. (Isn't that great???!!!)

Just read this slowly to yourself:

I forgive myself for the upheaval that this transition is causing.

I forgive myself for the upheaval that this transition is causing. And, I also forgive those that affected this transition. There are people or other conditions (even the darn calendar whose pages keep turning) that you could be angry at. And it is time to forgive them for what is becoming your new reality.

By forgiving the people or other circumstances that led to this transition, you acknowledge that they were and are important to you. You dive just that bit deeper into the grieving process. You allow just that bit more pressure to release. And, you can more readily bring love, or at least more peace, to your transition.

This also allows you to reflect on your path, giving it Grace, as well. Where have you been in the past decade? How did you get here? Are there things you wish you had or hadn't done? Sure... and yet, with peace, you can move through this phase.

That gut-wrenching sense of, "I should have..." or "If only..." from the Bargaining phase is left behind, as well. It becomes a calm existential look at *Self.* Having come through the other phases, having done this kind of pre-grieving work, you can look ahead to your next great chapter in your life with hopeful anticipation. You look ahead without regrets for what did or didn't happen, knowing that you had a decent ride anyway.

Is there more? Yes! There could have been more. There will always be more to do, to see, to create. And that is why looking ahead is so important. Go back to that place of feeling like you are giving a gift to those who come behind you. Perhaps their sense of "more" will pick up where yours left off.

And whose "more" are you stepping into now? There may be someone, somewhere who would be hoping they could do what <u>you</u> are about to do. Step forward without remorse or regret, knowing that you are boldly and gracefully about to take on the next great chapter of your life.

You've got this!

7

FEAR AND EXCITEMENT
OR EXCITEMENT AND FEAR

Excitement and fear are two different ends of a spectrum. One moves you forward, the other stops you where you are. Physiologically, the effects appear identical. For example, as you stare at a rollercoaster, your eyes dilate, your heart pounds just a little bit, and your pulse races. Your palms might even get a little bit sweaty. If you are excited about rollercoasters, you move forward with eager anticipation about the ride. If you are a person who is afraid of the ride, what you are feeling stops you in your tracks.

Transitions are very much like facing a roller coaster ride that you have only heard about. There is no way to pre-ride it other than to look at the climbs, drops, and loops that others have taken. Yet your ride, your engagement in it, and your reaction to it, will all be quite personal!

This is where the *psycho*logical meets the *physio*logical.

Excitement for the rollercoaster that is ahead of you means that your heart races just a little bit. Your eyes dilate, your pulse quickens, and your palms might just be a little bit sweaty in anticipation of the future.

For some, however, you look at the future with great trepidation. You worry about what dangers might lay in the darkness. Your fears grow. Your eyes dilate. Your heart races. Your palms probably become a little sweaty, and you are stopped in your tracks.

What is your mindset about the unknown? Do you choose to move forward with great excitement? Or, do you stop, frozen. Do you back away slowly and decide to turn around? Maybe, just maybe, you'll choose only to be a passive observer. Perhaps you will choose to not even watch at all.

At the whim of others' planning for you, are you choosing to simply, and docilely, stand on the sidelines? Some people do. In the face of difficult decisions, some people will choose not to participate or to delegate, but actually to abdicate, leaving the decision-making to family members, the government, or other outside circumstances.

When that happens, great bitterness arises. There is a sense of outrage that this was done *to* you. Feeling out of control creates a sense of anger and a sense of urgency. That need to do something, to do anything, can lead to overwhelm. This, in turn, can lead to giving up or giving in. This cycle is such that a feeling of helplessness ensues.

Where are you in the process? This is, after all, *your* process.

It is one thing to anticipate the sense of loss and feelings of letting go. It is quite another thing to anticipate all of the unknowns that lay ahead.

The unknown is that great rollercoaster that stands before us, looming largely in the not-so-distant future. We have left behind the question of "Who am I if I am not a _____?" We now engage in "What if _____?" (The blank filled in here with something treacherous). Our thoughts go to the scary, the ominous, the potential evils and pitfalls into which we might slide. Our thoughts turn to catastrophizing. Our nights become sleepless. Our days become filled with anxiety. And our nighttime reflections are filled with worry about the deep, dark void ... the unknown.

Do you have what it takes to venture forth? Some of the anxiety or the "stoppers" that linger, becoming somewhat free floating, converge around questions of "enough." You may wonder whether you are enough or whether you have enough or even whether you have prepared enough. All of these questions each have their own answers. The funny thing is, usually the answer comes out as twofold: "yes" and "it depends."

If you are planning a trip, let's say to California In June, you would do some research. You would want to know things like what attractions will be nearby, where you'd be staying, that kind of thing. You might want to know how much the attractions cost, how much your lodging would cost, or how much your food would cost. These would be approximate amounts, but you'd still want to know to inform future decisions.

There's a belief that in the summertime California gets quite warm. If you ended up in Fresno, for example, you might find yourself wanting to shed clothing because it is, in fact, quite warm. While Fresno Is not near the beach and you wouldn't be surfing or participating In water sports or activities, you would find yourself enjoying, baking, or sweltering in the sunshine.

On the other hand, if you were to take a trip to California and ended up in San Francisco, especially during the summertime, you would find yourself putting on more, and more, and more clothing. Mark Twain said that the coldest winter he ever spent was a summer in San Francisco. There's a reason for that: it does get cold. If you blindly assume that California is warm and delightful in the summer, you might be slightly surprised to find yourself baking in one area of California and freezing in another area.

This analogy is drawn out here to suggest that you do, in fact, need to do some research prior to launching into your future. To offset the questions of whether you are enough or have enough, the biggest question is, are you prepared internally?

Specifically, do you believe in yourself? Do you believe in your ability to rebound with resilience when the steps you intended to take do not go as planned?

When you answer the question of whether you have what it takes and you end up with a meek uncertainty, overwhelm heats up and anxiety stops your potential forward momentum. Then, the floodgates open as the "what if" questions gush forth in some awkward attempt to drown you.

Here is where you get to boost your psychology. While an anxious focus on the future creates apprehension that stops you in your tracks, you have other options that could flip your internal switch and allow you to move forward instead. Remember that anxiety, worry, and doubt are based on you investing energy in *imagining* a negative outcome about the future.

What would happen if you spent your energy imagining a brighter outcome and then actually planning for it? Let us dive in a little deeper here, because this relates to _any_ transition – whether from your career, from your family situation, or even "simply" moving (gracefully) from today to tomorrow. The bold question to ask yourself is this: What if you put your energy to a different use?

More specifically: Rather than investing your energy in worrying about a devastating imagined outcome, what if you invested in imagining a truly beautiful, peaceful, and positive outcome?

Fear, doubt, and worry turn to possibility. With a mindset shift and deliberate intent, the "what if" question becomes one that creates optimism. Rather than pausing to wallow in the momentum-stopping fear, remember that transitions are about moving across or crossing over from where you are to a new world for yourself. And, quite powerfully, it is one that you actually get to create.

While you have a broad inventory of the people, places, things, and activities that you are leaving behind, by creating new self-talk focused on the positive new prospects that lay ahead, your sense of loss begins to heal. You look again to possibilities for abundance, the way you did when your journey started so many years ago. Options exist. Worry turns to anticipation.

When you approach the unknown,
you have two options:

Withdrawal into Worry

or

Advance Into Curiosity

That's it. It really does come down to that.

We pause and withdraw for so many "reasons." Emotions overwhelm us in such a way that they *seem* logical. We look at what we are giving up, and go through the grieving stages. We become afraid of giving up the familiar. And in that fear, we stop our progress, wondering perhaps if it is worth it.

And it is the fear that stops us. If you made a New Year's resolution to "get healthier," somewhere you realize that you will be giving up certain favorites (different for everyone, but could include cookies, cake, pizza, chips, beer, etc.). While at a distance, letting go of those things seems logical and almost easy, the truth is that when they are a part of your life, they are comforting.

Letting them go creates a void. And again, it is that dark empty space that we are afraid of. We don't fear letting go. We fear not having something comforting and familiar in the dark empty space. It is the sense of "what will I do without that?" which stops us. We have pangs of withdrawal as even the thought of "not having" makes us want it more.

When you move on from a long-time career, you are left with the craving for what was familiar. The fear that creeps in, that feeling that stops you, is the overwhelming sense of questioning what you will do without that familiar, comforting role. You begin to feel that if you move forward, you will be creating a dark hole that you could simply fall into. And if that happened, you'd be gone.

The "you" that you knew will disappear. That really IS scary. Withdrawal from others happens. Push-back happens. Push-away happens. Anger happens. Depression happens. And the stages of grieving that loss begin to make much more sense.

We not only grieve, we are afraid of the emptiness that we create for ourselves.

You are likely facing the realization that making the shift is going to have some difficulty. That is, actually making the shift, the *process* of the transition, is itself, going to be hard. If you have ever moved-house or even just cleared something out of a room to paint it, you know that there is real work involved. Looking at the monumental task of moving from a career or relationship, for example, you face the reality of packing up years of actual and psychological luggage.

You look at what it will take to move them. You moan, "this is just… too… harrrrrrddddd…." And it is. It IS hard work to move. And the prospect of climbing that mountain of work could stop you. The internal moaning gets louder. It might even come squeaking out of you. Or such internal complaints might erupt loudly as anger or bargaining. And the grieving process makes itself known again.

Moving across from one place to a new place, the transition itself, IS hard work.

The pain of the loss can stop you. The work involved in making the move can stop you. And not knowing – the unkown absolute of an outcome – that can be frightening. And some people go there after grieving. You might wonder whether where you are going is actually better than where you were. (Hint: It is not better. Oh, and it is not worse, either. It IS different though. But not knowing what it IS can be a mental road block that stops forward progression.)

A fear of the outcome, THEN a fear of the process. This is where the concept of *Moving Across* really becomes apparent. You might have an image in mind of packing everything from your past, strapping it to your back, and climbing a mountain with it. Yes, this transition thing IS difficult, and you are hereby given permission to whine… for about three minutes. Whining does not, in actuality, get you anywhere. It feels good for a very short time.

If you get stuck there, overcoming inertia is more difficult than using the feelings associated with the knowledge of the difficulty for momentum. You know this mountain was going to be hard to climb when you started, but now your feet are stuck In mud.

This is psychological physics.

Getting out of being stuck takes more energy and effort than enduring the difficulty and continuing to move forward. Here, it will be important for you to keep moving forward, putting one foot in front of the other, step-by-step.

It IS hard. You get a medal for finishing a marathon. You don't have to come in first to get the medal. You just have to keep going, knowing that there is a finish line, even when it is not in sight.

Continuing with the analogy of the marathon, there comes a point at which–actually there are several points at which–the runner questions whether it is worth it. They look at giving up several areas of comfort simply to train for the marathon, running before the sun is up. Running on weekends. Aching afterwards. They get up early, having paid to gather with tens of thousands of other people doing the same thing.

The race ensues, and you show determination. Mile markers remind you of your progress, the way that the turning of the calendar pages offer acknowledgment. Sometimes those milestones provide for celebration and sometimes they suggest a treacherous future ahead. For many runners, three-quarters of the way through a long-distance race, a funny thing happens. The "big why" phenomenon strikes. The internal dialogue of "remind me why I'm doing this" pops up, and it becomes a matter of telling yourself to just keep moving, step-by-step.

Just keep moving. That works. Until you wonder whether it will all be worth it. You start to wonder whether where you are headed is going to be what you want. For the runner, it's just another medal. That seemed like a decent prize when you had the thought of entering the race. Now, it is just a little trinket that is so far away. And for you in transition, what if you get to where you are going and you really just do not like it? What if you get there, and it is not what you had imagined?

What if you get there and all you have is you?

Is it going to be worth it? The thing is, you will not actually know the answer to that until you get there. In reality, it is hard to let go of the familiar. There really IS a sense of loss, and you really WILL go through the grieving stages to a greater or lesser extent.

Making a move, any kind of move, does have its difficulties. There really IS hardship at some point. And what may be easy for some might be a stopper for you. Or vice-versa. Along the way, you will whine to yourself about how hard the process of the transition really is.

And the getting there is different than the being there. The wondering whether it is worth it is part of the withdrawal process. It is fear that causes you to step back instead of stepping in. And you cannot know the outcome until you actually create the outcome. And it is here that you push out of withdrawal and step forward with curiosity.

Your magical power is to turn "What if it's bad?" into a fun, fresh inquisitive approach of "I wonder what this will be like!" Engage and advance with curiosity. In fact, staying curious keeps you out of judgment!

When you are in curiosity, you cannot be in judgment!

Your future is yours to create. Putting creative, inquisitive energy into it actually draws you forward. Where energy is directed to creating something new, dopamine dumps, and a feeling of well-being takes over.

Wait. What? You have spent all of this time in worry, anger, and depression, and you could have been skipping and frolicking? Well, yes. The truth is that you will experience a wide range of emotions, all of which are valuable. And no, no one is expecting you to go skipping and frolicking out of your long-time career/relationship/lifestyle/etc. What you get to have at your disposal, though, is the knowledge that what you experience is truly up to you.

Some things bear repeating:

What you experience is truly up to you!

Two key elements will allow you to move quickly through the not-so-pleasant and into the "Wow! I can't wait."

What key elements make the transition easier? You will be surprised.

First, PLAN.

Rarely does anyone make a major life move without a plan. Previously we talked about how looking ahead lets you know what to expect (it really is cold in San Francisco in the summer, so pack for that) and how doing so enables you to overcome obstacles along the way.

The best time to have a map is before you go into the forest.

Planning helps you know what to look out for. It also helps you know what to look forward to. So much energy goes into worry and overcoming obstacles and not enough goes into planning for the adventure and fun that comes with doing something new. Staying curious will keep you out of judgment. Planning will help you build some wonderful and new experiences into your days ahead.

What will you explore? How will you find what you need? Whom will you contact first? Planning for what you are looking forward to will draw you into the future with excitement and anticipation rather than facing anxiety and fear. Moving forward toward this rollercoaster that looms so largely ahead, you begin to wonder how much fun this ride will give you! Yes, there will be a rush and some exhilaration… if you let it in.

The other key element that will move you forward is the magic inside any transition: resilience. Knowing that you can and will bounce back from pretty much anything allows you to step forward with confidence. Look, you're the oldest you've ever been. That means that something you have done along the way has led you to be here.

Take inventory – you have bounced back many, many times. You have endured loss. You have endured embarrassment. You have endured heartache. And you are not the only one to do so. Not only are you capable, you are not alone!

That is sometimes a huge revelation.

The magic element in your transition is your ability to be resilient!

You have been and you are! Remind yourself that you are capable. Remind yourself that you have a plan. Remind yourself that the plan does NOT show all of the details. It cannot do so. On a long road trip, you cannot predict which rest stops will have availability or not. You can predict approximately when you will stop for a refresh.

And it is that, your ability to be flexible and resilient, your ability to engage with curiosity and wonder, that will propel you toward a bold and graceful transition.

Today, for example – today… what new and wonderful thing will you explore? It does not have to be some grand adventure. Simply, practice this: What one new thing can I do today, exploring with genuine curiosity without judgment?

Stay curious.

Know that you will bounce back!

And as always, be sure to go to www.DynamicTransitions .com/bonus

Enjoy!

8

A LIGHT IN THE DARKNESS

In the last chapter, you got a chance to look at what it means to move forward boldly but awkwardly or to be stopped by the fear and anxiety surrounding the unknown. To better break through, a plan provides the torch to illuminate the darkened tunnel. And with a little curiosity, rather than withdraw, you are drawn into the future, *your* future!

Some people are afraid to voice their wishes or plans out loud for fear that doing so will cause them to be changed or jinxed. In actuality, bringing your plans out for all to see allows you greater levels of influence. The main thing you need when you have a plan is not approval from others, but rather, confidence. As you then share your plans, you gain support from others.

Your PLAN is your declaration of direction!

And just wait until you DO share your plans—everyone will have something to say about them. Because there will be no shortage of opinions and advice, your ability to be both curious and clear counts tremendously. Certainly, you would like to learn from others who are experts. That said, you will have your own opinions based on your previous research and based on your true desires. It matters that you are clear about your direction. It also matters that your direction is based on your values.

Mothers-to-be understand this all too well. Unfortunately, their transition into parenthood is pretty much announced for them. Why is it that the advice to pregnant women seems to come with stories of tragedy and hardship? Why is it that women do not support each other on the road to new parenthood by saying things like, "this is going to be wonderful" or reassuring the pregnant mom-to-be that she is going to do great?

Are all adventures and transitions filled with stories of tragedy? "Oh, you don't know what you're in for!" Or, "Well, now life as you know it is over." Both of those statements are true; but they are not necessarily the message of doom. Knowing in advance that others will offer information and guidance that has been wrapped in a layer of poo means you get to choose whether to accept the "gift" of advice or not.

Not all gifts need to be accepted. Free advice is just that, and sometimes its value is less than that. Focus instead on your plan and your purpose which give you the lenses you need to see through the intent of the advice that is being offered. Do they mean well, or do they mean to make themselves feel better about having done something differently than you?

Stand firm, reminding yourself that you do have a plan. Take solace in the fact that your plan provides a foundation for your declaration of direction. What some people miss is that if you bring your plan into the darkness of the unknown, the plan isn't changed because of the unknown. In fact, it is the unknown that is changed by the plan. It is the darkness that is altered by the light, and not the other way around.

Bringing a lit candle into the dark doesn't change the candle or the flame.

The perspective you need is to remember that darkness is not the presence of dark, but rather the absence of light. And so, transitioning to an unknown space is not that the unknown is full of darkness, but rather that it is absent the lightness of your plan. Get clear about your direction before announcing your intention. Wistful musings are not declarations of direction. "Gosh, maybe I'll just go and live off the land for a while." That's different than, "I'm selling my home and buying a farm where I can actually cultivate the food I eat." Having clarity and creating a declaration based on that clarity is what it means to bring the light to the dark.

Corporate and entrepreneurial clients will start with the exercise of understanding their values as the first step along the way to creating a vision for their future. Your earlier exercises in this book allowed you an insight about what you valued in the past. We will return to touch on those shortly. What *was*, mattered. What *IS* matters more.

Clarity of direction *IS* your light! Holding that torch, then ask yourself, what does it take to venture forth? The answer comes back to Curiosity and Courage! Recognizing that you can actually muster these—as in, YOU call them forth—you get to a place where fear deliberately turns to excitement.

When you call up curiosity, judgment (including self-judge-ment) abates. Truly being curious about your future leaves you with an almost child-like wonder. You get to explore rather than having to forge new trails for yourself. Work turns to play, and your life's path becomes lighter.

This is where the bold meets the graceful, as you step firmly into your transition. By exploring with a lighter heart, you open yourself to more possibility. Yes, you are clear about your direction. And yes, your eyes are open to exploring the new. A plan doesn't mean that everything is accounted for; if you're going on a picnic you must not count on nine ants crossing your blanket at 1:37 p.m. People like that exist, and their lives are miserable, because what happens is that only six ants cross the blanket and the whole picnic becomes ruined.

Instead, the plan is to have a picnic, to bring certain items with you, to buy certain items, and to find a nice place to sit. Exploration is built into the plan. Rigidity is a way to be miserable in your life. You end up blaming the world around you for not conforming to the circumstances you have created. Lighten up. Stay curious. Bring your own sense of wonder to everything you do. And as you do, smile every now and then. This transitions stuff can actually be fun!

Remember that rollercoaster analogy? When fear turns to excitement, that can be a deliberate switch. In fact, think about anything small you just *have to* get done in your day today. There's some tedium to that. "I have to do the dishes" or "I have to write that report." When you deliberately/intentionally change that *have to* into *get to*, your whole approach changes. And so does the outcome. "I get to eat off of clean dishes later and I get to have a clear countertop and sink" is so different from facing the drudgery of a chore looming largely. "I get to move this from my in-box and pass it to someone else who will get to turn this information into something larger for our company." That's so much more fulfilling than, "I have to write this report."

The reason it is important to practice being deliberate and intentional is to demonstrate to yourself that you, only you, have control of your psychology. Your mindset is something that you control. You have the power to take a "have to" situation and turn it into a "get to" situation. You have the power to turn a fear into some form of excitement based on curiosity.

In <u>Choosing Your Power</u>, the concept of your Envisioned Positive Outcome was illustrated. When you can think about where you are headed and what that means in terms of creating a positive space, your path to get there is so much clearer and a whole lot more meaningful. People spend a lot of time catastrophizing about the future. If you know what you don't want, but aren't so clear about what you do want, then at least, for a start, quarantine the "don't want" stuff.

Be intentional. Turn what felt like fear into excitement. Practice that every day. In fact, practice that whenever you feel the burden of "ughhh, I have so much to do" sweep over you. As fear fades and excitement takes over, then energy returns. The concept of fight or flight stems from both of these, being fear-based responses, when you feel like you are out of options.

Instead, remember that you have choices all around you. When you enter that place of wonder, not blowing in the wind at someone else's whim, but having your plan and then engaging in curiosity with it, you move from fight or flight into excitement, and a sense of "Heck, yeahhhhh!" moves you forward. It drives you forward.

You have control of your mindset. Be intentional!

Have you ever felt like you knew what needed to be done, but you were just too tired to do it? Yeah, that goes back to the "it's tooooo harrrrddddd" whining thing we get into, mentioned a little while ago. When it feels too hard and you really just do not feel driven, that means you are not clear. Think about the times you were absolutely certain about what outcome you wanted. There have been times that nothing could stop you. Oh, it IS hard, but nothing was going to stop you from reaching your outcome.

That ninth mile on a half-marathon is where you look back and exclaim, "Look how far I've come. That's not a bad warm up for a little four-mile run." Do you think fire-fighters look at burning buildings and decide that it might be too hard to tackle? They go in, knowing that there is a better outcome at the end! And if your child were behind a fire-line? The question of "too hard" would never come up.

No, you wouldn't stop because being super-clear on your values and your outcomes gives you energy. You get a strong drive to complete when you have clarity about where you are headed and what values-filters you will use along the way.

> *A greater sense of vitality comes from having a strong sense of clarity about your direction as you continue looking through the lenses of your values.*

Refer back to chapter three where you listed your roles and your values.

In creating a plan for forward movement and for looking forward, you will want to project your roles and your values into the future. As with personal development of any kind, look ahead and ask yourself this key question:

Who do I really want to become in the next decade or two?

Once you know who you want to become, then you begin putting the pieces in place to become just that. It might be simpler to start with these questions:

Projecting ahead twenty years, how do I want to look back on my life and how do I want to be remembered?

Create a plan for which values you will have and how you might exhibit them over time:

What Roles Will You Play and for whom over the next two decades?

Start with **This Week** – **What Roles Will You Play and for whom?**

Consider each arena you addressed earlier: Self, Family, Social, Financial, Professional, Physical, and Spiritual. Yes, you have just seven spaces here. Please feel free to use more paper or actually open your journal.

A)

B)

C)

D)

E)

F)

G)

Following are very specific times identified for you to look at. It will be important for you to wrap your head around where you will be and how you are choosing to develop yourself in each of these areas. It is possible that the people who were reliant upon you just ten years ago will be the ones to provide you some support twenty years out. Knowing what to expect and having a plan for your transitions over time will help you to stay vibrant and not succumb to what may feel like surprises. Will you need the same type of vehicle you do now? Will you want to spend more or less time doing a particular activity? Okay, so you've spent some time looking at just this week.

Now, look ahead in time!

What Roles Will You Play and for whom at this point next year? One year out, who are you becoming?

Again, consider each arena you addressed earlier: Self, Family, Social, Financial, Professional, Physical, and Spiritual. Given that you have just seven spaces here, be sure to use more paper or jot notes in your journal.

A)

B)

C)

D)

E)

F)

G)

That's right, one year from now you will be a different human with different relationships than you have right now. You will be in different physical shape. You will be in a different financial place. And you will have different family and friends around you. You might be more or less involved in raising children, your job, or in charity. These are the things to be thinking about as you move forward, as well.

And now we project ahead a bit more. This is a GREAT exercise for you no matter at what stage you are in your career development or lifespan.

What Roles Will You Play and for whom at this point in THREE Years? Over that time who are you becoming? Who will you need to become to say that these three years have been successful?

Continue to consider each arena you addressed earlier: Self, Family, Social, Financial, Professional, Physical, and Spiritual. Because there are only seven spaces here, you are encouraged to use more paper and make notes in your journal.

A)

B)

C)

D)

E)

F)

G)

You are doing great IF you have actually paused long enough to make some notes about your thoughts. Remember that planning is what provides you the ability to make a declaration. That gives you the influence you need and the vibrant energy you will want to lean into the next decade.

So leap ahead a little. From one week out, to a year, to three years—you could do this for the five-year mark, but instead, jump out ten years. How old will you be in ten years? Who

will you have around you? How will you be at home and in the
community?

What Roles Will You Play and for whom at this point in TEN Years?

Over that time who are you becoming?

Here, each area becomes even more significant to address. Be
certain you are making notes about the role you will play with
each of the following: Self, Family, Social, Financial, Professional, Physical, and Spiritual. The specific lines for each have
been eliminated here. Take your time. In a decade, what is
changing for you? Jot notes here and be sure to open your journal for this one.

Go! Right here, write here!

Do the exact same process for twenty years out. That's right, two decades from now, who will you be? Where will you be living? What contributions will you be making? To whom will you be connected?

Make notes about your role(s) and the values you will have twenty years from now.

What Roles Will You Play and for whom at this point in TWENTY Years? Over that time who are you becoming? How will you be at home and in the community?

Be sure to address the roles you are playing in the world and the values you are carrying forward or embodying. In twenty years, you will have changed significantly. The world will have advanced in ways you cannot even imagine. So who do you want to or need to become?

Focus on the roles and values you have for:

SELF

FAMILY

SOCIAL

FINANCIAL

PROFESSIONAL

PHYSICAL

SPIRITUAL

Yes, you are certainly going to want to spend some time in your journal for this one.

This is a big, bold step. Having some clue about who you want to be, and how you want to be will help you to define the steps to take to manifest that future for yourself.

Your plan creates a light for you to project and to follow!

While that may seem a bit magical, going through the exercises of clarity lays the solid groundwork needed now to support the future YOU. You have a bright future ahead. Having a plan helps to burn through the clouds looming above. The darkened sky brightens as you illuminate your path. No one else can truly show you the way. Your plan creates a light for you to both project as well as to follow.

If you have not yet done the exercises on the previous pages, pause now to do them. Really. Don't just think it in your head. Write your answers out.

If you DID just complete all of that, congratulations. You are probably feeling a little energy surge go through you. That vital flood will also help you feel much more relaxed. It is an odd paradox – you will be energized and calm at the same time. Instead of being the animal that has been pushed into a corner, you are more like the playful puppy or kitten ready to pounce.

You have a new-found clarity about who you are and what you are taking forward. Your drive is surging again; with a renewed vitality you step forward, ***boldly.***

As a wise fortune cookie once proclaimed, "Decisions Terminate Panic." A plan provides the power for bold movement and calm resolve. Energy returns, and the courage to take the next step percolates forth.

You may also take inventory. The path to courage, true courage, is to recognize that you have what it takes to make it through the next phase. Acknowledge the path you have been on and celebrate the steps you have already taken to get here. And with a keen understanding that what got you here won't get you there, you now look ahead to the steps you need to take.

By employing key attributes of getting clear about what matters to you (both in terms of values and the roles you play in the world), and by making a declaration about your direction, you create a certainty that you then blend with flexibility and resilience. This is what it takes to step forward, boldly and courageously. This is what it takes to bring a new vitality into your life.

There is more for you out there. There is so much more!

And you are making this journey happen by taking bold, courageous steps.

That's magical!

9

A NEW DAY

Getting clear and making a declaration about your path does, in fact, create an energetic pull into your now bright future. With a renewed energy for an envisioned brighter future ahead, you now eagerly embrace the newness. This could actually be fun! And it is from that perspective that the graceful part of the transition begins to engage.

Certainly, you may move ahead with a given dignity. You could hold your face firm and your eyes fixed. You take a stiffened step and then another step, equally as stiff. There is dignity in doing so. You deny that you are affected by any loss, stuck in the grieving process and daring to show very little.

Yet dignity is different than grace. As one moves boldly forward, uncovering new finds along the way, the release of tension is what brings grace. Grace also comes from gently acknowledging the past, holding it dearly as a fond memory. You hold the memory, embrace it where appropriate, and release it when necessary. That is true grace.

Dignity Is Different Than Grace

Remember that to have a truly *dynamic transition*, there is energy involved. Remember also that a transition is the action of *moving over or moving across* to something new. And today is a new day. You are leaning into the future with gleeful anticipation, having let go of the past that no longer encumbers you.

Given that this is a new day, you now look ahead to contributing productively and meaningfully. You take your values with you as you focus on what would make you feel good as well as what might make a difference in the world. Remember that plan you were making? It becomes all the more important here.

Just as your plan is your declaration of your direction, it also represents your honor in the world. What? Yes; your plan lets others know what you value and how you plan on drawing from or contributing to the resources of the (global) community. Your plan is your torch lighting the way. You will get lost without a plan. And you will get lost without feeling like you are doing what matters.

You have become clear about your direction. Energy surged back. Now, you take your newly revitalized self into the space of service. Remember, sometimes it really is okay to have a plan that is in service of the *Self*. This is not the time to become lackadaisical. No, here you must be directed. Even if your transition is into retirement, having a deliberate and intentional plan for your day makes a huge difference.

Productivity is about planning your day with specific outcomes in mind

Knowing what you want to get out of your day allows you to plan for what you want to put into your day. This is not a state of "inflate my balloon." The people who engage in the world like that are living a life of dissatisfaction and blame. And by getting this far in your Dynamic Transition, you are *not* that person!

What is your big "why" for the "what" and "how" of your day? Partly, you are engaging in service to your *Self* and to others to prove to your psyche that you, the inner soul *you*, still matter.

You Still Matter!

By now, that should be evident. The doubt and fear-laden question of "Who am I if I'm not a _____?" softly shifts to the more driven and resolute question of "Who am I becoming and how might I serve others differently than I have in the past?"

Even if your transition is not a comparatively large one, it is worth asking that question of yourself, perhaps every day! *Who am I becoming and how might I serve others differently than I have in the past?* No matter what stage of life you are in, you have the ability to offer those coming up behind you something of value. You have experience, insight, and perspective that they do not have.

Mentoring and eldering are places to step in to offer others the insights from the hard-fought lessons you learned along your path. For whom might your wisdom be valuable?

Seriously. Reflect on that for a bit. To whom could you offer significant advice and counsel so that their lives might be better? When you think this way, your legacy comes to life! Remember that it really does not matter what phase of life you are in. The transitions – plural – that you have endured and survived have taught you things that others would find of value.

Mentorship might be one part of your plan. It might not be any part of your plan. The main concept to hold onto here is that you actually _have_ a plan! Here, the key is that you move into a new sense of productivity. Your meaning and your significance (see The Significance Factor) shifts as you step into a new kind of service, be that to self or to others.

Communicating your plan makes a difference in whether it will come to fruition or not, as well. There are three Cs at work here. The first is Clarity – you are clear about your direction now.

The second is Communication – you now must not assume that others know what you want. Your desires have to be communicated clearly. Only in so doing can you expect support for your new direction. It is in clarity and communication that you can garner support and have sway in your newly developing relationships.

This is influence. You step into a new relationship guiding the way, collaborating and co-creating, as your desires and direction become clearly known. Getting support for your new goals and dreams means changing the way you engage in what feels like a new, sometimes awkward relationship.

This is not unusual. As one person in the dynamic relationship shifts his or her role in the world, that person has to establish a new identity related to (but not bound to) that new role. The other partner and family members shift as the new identity emerges.

This is not a wholesale swapping out of one personality for another. Rather, this is the formation of a new personal identity tied to the roles that are being grown into. Remember that a relationship is not static. In fact, the very nature of _any_ relationship is that it is dynamic.

As partners, family members, and/or teams come together anew, the Latin roots of the word _relationship_ mean the state of coming together again. And by being explicit in your wants and needs, by clearly stating your plan, and by inviting others to join you, your level of influence climbs. That is, the likelihood becomes much higher that you will get the outcome that you desire because you have clearly enlisted the support of those around you.

Is it possible that you can (and do) create a new you? Yes! Yes, it is. Every day is a new day, and we each create the new "me" that we step into. Will you be more bold or courageous? Will you be more giving? Will you be more adventurous? That is all completely up to you.

EVERY Day is a New Day and A New Day = A New You

But who am I to be today? Who am I? That is the existential dilemma, isn't it! The real question as we transition boldly and gracefully into the next great chapter of our lives is just that:

Who Am I To Be Today?

Isn't that a great question? You get to choose who you are and who you are becoming every day! Yes, every… single… day! When you carry forward your core values, you can awaken with gratitude and then spring into the day with intent and direction!

You're given this day! How will you fill it?

When you engage in the world intentionally, you know what you will bring to your day. Quite simply, knowing *that* extinguishes the existential dilemma! The questions of *"Who am I?"* or *"Who am I to be?"* no longer have a dark cloud connotation. The storm is not moving in.

In fact, these questions become quite positive. And, because you might have been keeping track, the third of the three Cs (Clarity and Communication being the first two) is that of Curiosity. Yes, as you lean in, you engage in your future with a renewed sense of wonder. Staying curious about *how* you will be *who* you will be brings a renewed vitality once again.

This is like an infinite loop. You gain vitality by having clarity. That means that your strong sense of self and sense of direction help you feel more alive. You take that feeling of really being alive and focus it forward. You step into your new day, each day, and you wonder (with a smile on your face) who am I to be today?

Can you feel that? Stepping out of dread, can you feel the relief that wonder brings? You may even wryly look back and begin asking the question, "Who did I think I was?" You clearly know you are not that any more. Have you ever looked back at photos from several decades ago? You wonder what were people thinking, dressing like that or acting like that. These questions become all the more profound when you find yourself in one of those photos.

Huhhhh... Who did I think I was?

Time sets the context for the answer to that question. We each do the best we can with what we have at the time. We follow – or push away from – fads. We seek desperately to fit in while struggling to stand out. That is a lot of work.

As you engage in your Dynamic Transition, you take on the challenge of being graceful and sliding into the next great phase of your life. You also accept the challenge of being bold, knowing that what others think of you is not of consequence.

We seek desperately to fit in while struggling to stand out

The challenge to be both bold and graceful in your transition requires your ability to engage all of your talents and every exercise that you have engaged in during your reading of this book. Knowing your values helps you grow them in this next great phase of your life. It is here that you truly build the bridge to the future.

In some cultures (such as the U.K.), being "bold" is not something desirable. In the context of this book, certainly you have picked up that bold could mean intrepid, pioneering a new way with unwavering confidence. Can you be that? Can you show yourself a new way confidently? Knowing who you are and what you value allows you to do so!

What about being graceful in your time of transition? When you think of graceful as Grace-full, you have a slightly new meaning and new context. Showing grace for your former self and your former circumstances allows you not only to let go, but to look ahead with a sense of calm confidence.

You look ahead. You take calm confidence with you. And, you show others the Way. That is the Way of the Dynamic Transitions!

And so you go, boldly and gracefully forward into the next great chapter of your life. Will you have doubts? Yes. And do you know why? Because you are human, and you cannot know the outcome of your adventure with absolute certainty. Certainly, one outcome is clear. We all get there eventually. What matters now is how you fill the time between now and the inevitable.

How? Boldly.

How? Gracefully!

With each tick of the clock and with each breath you take, something changes. Something dies. Something new emerges. And this might scare you, even now. One question to keep in mind is this: Where would you be in a year, or two, or three if you *didn't* take this path? The reality is, the adventure that lays before you is your yellow brick road. This is your adventure. There are steps to be taken. And... you must now take them! You *may* now take them. Enjoy!

And remember your resources at www.DynamicTransitions .com/Bonus

END NOTES

Dynamic Transitions are as much about the crossing over, the getting there, as they are about the place that you will land. This is the adventure: Dynamic Transitions – Moving Boldly and Gracefully Into The Next Great Phase Of Your Life

On this journey of Dynamic Transitions (www.Dynamic Transitions.com) you have endured and then embraced Crossing Over. You determined from where and to where. You assessed what you valued. You assessed what you now value. And you decided upon whom you will now become, leaving behind – and grieving for – that identity that you grew into, through, and out of.

It all starts with an idea of "what if?" and from there the ride begins. You choose a date and begin to wonder what you have done. You take a somewhat blind first step and then create a plan.

To make it all work, you must communicate that plan. That's how you garner support. You acknowledge the past and stay curious about the future, all the while staying curious and open to what may come. Your confidence grows as clarity develops.

Another step forward is taken. You recognize that YOU own your day and your future.

You might also recognize that your future begins now. And it is for that reason that we are perpetually in transition. For the seeds that we plant now take some time to germinate, to emerge, and to grow fully.

You own your day!

You own your future!

That gives you something to smile about. And you now move boldly ahead, honoring the past and embracing the future.

This is Dynamic Transitions: Moving Boldly And Gracefully Into The Next Great Phase Of Your Life!

ABOUT THE AUTHOR

 r. Wayne Pernell brings almost four decades of experience as a world-class high performance advisor to entrepreneurs and executives. Known as "The Leaders' Leader," Dr Pernell's expertise in relationships, leadership, and transitions has him in high demand.

His DynamicLeader® programs each provide a new perspective leveraging clarity and creating new strategic pathways for greater personal and professional wins in the world.

Dr Pernell has been seen in Forbes, on Fox and NBC morning television, and is an internationally acclaimed and best-selling Author, Speaker, and Certified High Performance Coach. His work has helped thousands of people across the globe.

Choosing Your Power, his first book, led Dr. Pernell to become a Hay House Featured Author and it continues to receive international acclaim. His second book, a best-seller written with Brian Tracy, The Winning Way, dives into the concept of Meaning Maker Leadership. He draws on the principles in this writing to lead his clients through key developmental steps for his exclusive mastermind programs.

His latest #1 Best-Selling book, The Significance Factor (September 2016), focuses on key steps every individual needs to take to transform their life of success to one that truly makes a difference. (To access these books, see www.WaynePernell .com/books.)

"Dr P" – as he is known by friends and associates – has a weekly blog (www.WaynePernell.com/blog) focusing on personal and professional development entitled, Wednesdays With Wayne. And his online courses have been hit as well. In fact, part of Dr P's personal mission statement is to teach, touch, and positively transform the lives of others. That is why he continues to create content related to personal and professional development focusing on relationships, leadership, and transitions. (A full menu of Dr Pernell's offerings can be found at www.WaynePernell.com.)

After earning his doctorate in clinical psychology, Dr. Pernell diverted from the traditional path of his peers and began working with organizational leaders and their teams. He has helped leaders in several high-profile companies including Schwab, 3Com, Whole Foods Market, AAA, and Simplex-Grinnell. Having grown up as the son of a dentist, Dr Pernell circled back to help dental professionals level up their game. In addition to growing his DynamicLeader® programs, he has been with the Pride Institute since 2005 and now, as a Senior Consultant and the Director of Organization Development and, Dr P (as he's known by his clients and friends) continues to focus on leadership development, relationships, and transitions, helping his clients to break through to even greater success.

This man of many talents is no stranger to the stage. In addition to coaching and advising individuals and organizations, speaking, and training groups of all sizes internationally, Dr. Pernell is an accomplished magician, having performed locally and across the world to the amazement and delight of audiences of all ages. While not actually performing magic any more, you're likely to see something magical in everything he brings your way.

And yes, there's more. He's a fourth-degree black belt in Bushido, a multi-disciplinary martial art (meaning "the Way of the warrior"). For three decades, he taught students to continually assess what options are available so that conflict can be minimized or eliminated. Drawing on these concepts, Sensei Wayne helps his clients (and his readers) get through tough spots and reduce conflict in their lives by emphasizing that true freedom comes from awareness of choice, even during extremely high-pressure situations.

Put all that together and you can be assured you're in good hands. You'll want to reach out to connect with Dr Wayne Pernell as he continues to achieve break-through levels of personal and professional success with his clients engaging in one of his world-class programs. It's no wonder he has become known as The Leaders' Leader!

www.DynamicTransitions.com

BONUS FOR READERS!

There are some great bonuses available for you at www. DynamicTransitions.com/bonus
        Be sure to head there to download your bonus workbook.

You will also find a couple of other great things there for you. Some bonus relationship material, coupon codes, and updates on things that will really help to move you forward in your life. Sure some of these are advanced, but I have created shortcuts for you so that you can step into them pretty easily.

Take a look and let me know what you think!

Links for you to click on (hit ALL of them)!!!

1) www.DynamicTransitions.com/bonus
2) www.WaynePernell.com – look around at the books and courses, get your free weekly Wednesdays With Wayne blog, too!
3) www.Facebook.com/WaynePernell - see you there!
4) https://www.linkedin.com/in/waynepernell/

5) www.Twitter.com/WaynePernell
6) And yes, subscribe to my YouTube channel and never miss a quick two-minute inspirational video www.YouTube.com /WaynePernell

Get your bonuses and be sure to connect with me! It's that easy! I look forward to your growth, development, and next big phase of your life.

35123378R10066

Made in the USA
Middletown, DE
02 February 2019